To My Teenager

I want you to keep these words
*   close to your heart.*
I want them to guide you
*   on your beautiful journey.*
I want you to be reminded
*   of how very much you are loved*
and know that no matter where you are
*   or where life takes you,*
I am with you every step of the way.

Elle Mastro

...AND HOME WILL ALWAYS BE HERE FOR YOU

———◇◇◇———

There's no greater place on earth
than the inside of a house
filled with those who make home
everything it's meant to be.
It's where memories are made
from the warmth of smiles,
spontaneous hugs, caring hearts,
and those who are remembered
with love.

———————

Barbara J. Hall

Remember that home will always be home for
    you, regardless of where life takes you.
The door will always be left open to you
With love that will continue to grow as you grow,
    just as it always has throughout your life.

———————

Susan Hickman Sater

What Every Parent Wants Their Teenager to Know

Your happiness, health, and safety
mean everything to me.

No matter how old you get,
I will always think of you as my child
and love you as much as ever.

I enjoy being with you
and am very pleased at the person
you've turned out to be.

Your voice is one of my favorite sounds,
and your laughter always delights me.

You should always believe
that you are capable and worthy,
precious and unique —
    and act accordingly.

For My

Teenager

A Blue Mountain Arts® Collection

Filled with a Little Bit of Wisdom and a Whole Lot of Love

Edited by Diane Mastromarino

Blue Mountain Press™

Boulder, Colorado

ACKNOWLEDGMENTS appear on page 48.

Certain trademarks are used under license.

Manufactured in the United States of America.

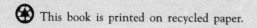 This book is printed on recycled paper.

Blue Mountain Arts, Inc.
P.O. Box 4549, Boulder, Colorado 80306

Contents

(Authors listed in order of first appearance)

For You, My Teenager, with All My Love

Sometimes I look at you
and I still see a vision
of the child you once were.
A smile surrounded by
chocolate ice cream,
knees covered with
scrapes and bruises,
feet that never stopped moving,
always carrying you from
one adventure to the next.
It's amazing to stand back
and realize how much you've grown.
The changes that took place
so gradually over the years
now make me stop and catch my breath...
my child, no longer a child,
all grown-up and ready to face the world.

I just want you to know
how proud I am of you.
With each new accomplishment you make,
my heart feels ready to burst with joy.
You've become all that I imagined
and so much more.
You've grown into such a wonderful person,
so caring and giving, confident, and brave.
One day I hope you'll be able to understand
all that I'm feeling in my heart...
but for now,
I just hope you can understand
how very much
I love you.

Carol Thomas

I Am So Proud of You
and the Way
You Have Chosen
to Conduct Your Life

I often marvel at your strength
to not give in to current misguided
morals and trends
and I know it is hard to be an individual
in a world of followers
where it is easy to go along with the crowd
Unfortunately, many people just get
swept up into certain types of behavior
which carries them from age to age
without any creative thought

It is so important for people
to actually choose the way to
    conduct their lives
And because you have done this
your relationships and accomplishments
will be genuinely deserved
and you will always
stand apart from the crowd
You will make a difference
in the world
with your dreams and actions
and I am so proud of you

———————————
Susan Polis Schutz

Don't Ever Let Anything Stand in the Way of Your Dreams

Catch the star that holds your destiny —
the one that forever twinkles
    within your heart
Take advantage of precious opportunities
while they still sparkle before you
Always believe that your ultimate goal
is attainable as long as you commit
    yourself to it

Though barriers may sometimes
stand in the way of your dreams
remember that your destiny
    is hiding behind them
Accept the fact that not everyone
is going to approve of the choices
    you make
but have faith in your judgment

Catch the star that twinkles in your heart
and it will lead you to your destiny's path
Follow that pathway and uncover the
    sweet sunrises that await you

Take pride in your accomplishments
as they are steppingstones
    to your dreams
Understand that you may
    make mistakes
but don't let them discourage you
Value your capabilities and talents
for they are what make you truly unique

The greatest gifts in life are not purchased
but acquired through hard work
    and determination
Find the star that twinkles in your heart
for you are capable of making
your brightest dreams come true
Give your hopes everything you've got
and you will catch the star
    that holds your destiny

Shannon M. Lester

BE BEAUTIFUL...

There is beauty in so many
unrecognized places.
It's a different beauty
than you find in magazines
that become the same face
    page after page.
It's not so much about
shapes or fabrics
    or cut and color.

Beauty is in how you invite
people into your life
and your heart no matter what.
It's when you laugh and cry
    with your whole self
just because that's how you feel.

Beauty is the way you move
when you think no one
    is watching
and you forget the shadows
of the "shoulds" and "supposed-to's."

Beauty is courage, energy,
    hope, and grace.
Beauty is you...
    just as you are.

Sue Gillies-Bradley

...BY BEING YOU

Throughout life
you will walk many paths
meet many people
and experience many things
Don't ever try to change
the person you are
to meet someone else's needs
Be yourself —
Never stop caring about the
things you value in life
and never stop striving to be
   your best

———————
Deana Marino

Instead of trying to fit yourself
into someone else's idea of perfection...
ask yourself:
   "What makes me happy?"

And when you have an answer,
your life begins to fit itself to your dreams.

———————
Amy Oscar

LOVE YOURSELF...

———◇◇◇———

Love each and every single part that makes you, you...
from your little pinky toe to your great big mind and
all those other parts in between. Make a conscious effort
to pat yourself on the back sometimes, and shower yourself
with praise every single day. There's no one who deserves
it more than you.

Diane Mastromarino

You must always love yourself. Give your mind good
thoughts. Give your body good nourishment and
exercise. Give your spirits good poetry, music, and
healthy doses of laughter. Give your soul the serenity
and healing of prayer.

Jacqueline Schiff

...AND SURROUND YOURSELF WITH THOSE WHO LOVE YOU

———◇◇◇———

Some people will be your friend
because of whom you know
Some people will be your friend
because of your position
Some people will be your friend
because of the way you look
Some people will be your friend
because of your possessions
But the only real friends
are the people who will be your friends
because they like you for how you are inside

Susan Polis Schutz

Keep away from people who try to belittle your ambitions.
Small people always do that, but the really great make you
feel that you, too, can become great.

Mark Twain

WE'LL ALWAYS
BE A FAMILY...

A family is people joined in love.
People who support each other through the good and
the bad times.
People who create a safe haven for the ones they love.
People who only want the best for each other.
People guided by the understanding and quiet acceptance
of those they love.

A family is people who are open, giving, and committed
to each other's well-being and the bonds between them.
People joined and strengthened by the love they have for
each other.
People who would do anything to make everything okay
for the ones they love.

A family is the love in our hearts...
forever.

Linda Sackett-Morrison

You have touched my heart
and made me proud
more often than you could imagine.

Memories of you are very dear to me,
and sharing special times and traditions
makes them all the more enjoyable.

You bless my life in so many ways,
and I am thankful for the friendship
that we share.

There is nothing you could ever do
to lessen my love for you.

Being your parent has given me
happiness to the greatest degree,
and warmth that fills my heart.
I am in awe that you came into my life
and made my dreams come true.

Barbara Cage

The World Changed
the Day You Were Born

The sun became brighter
The sky turned a soulful
   shade of blue
The air was cleaner
   and the grass greener
Smiles became broader
   laughter louder
Love grew stronger and deeper
Hearts swelled with humble pride
   thankful that God had blessed
      our family.

As you grew, I was there
   helping and watching
wiping away tears, easing little hurts
applauding increased accomplishments
and enjoying the performance
   of the day

As time passed, I stepped back
making way for the space you required
I marveled at your growth
and reveled in the fine young person
maturing in front of my very eyes

Now you stand ready
to move forward even more
a great big challenging world
    awaits you
one full of hopes and dreams —
a world that you *already* made better...
    the day you were born

———————
James E. Smith

Words to Remember...

Remember that reaching your destination is only part of living. Enjoying the journey is the other.

Remember that no one person in life can make you happy. True happiness comes from within.

Remember that words are very powerful, and they stay around forever — so always make sure that what you say counts.

Remember that true love is the most precious gift of all and the most tender of all emotions. Be sure to give it out as much as possible.

Remember that no one has all the answers to life. Life is an adventure that must be enjoyed to the fullest. Sometimes it is the surprises along the way that make it all worthwhile.

Remember to be kind to the strangers you meet along your path. You never know how they might touch your life.

Remember that if today seems dark, tomorrow may be brighter. Sometimes we need to get lost in the darkness before we can fully appreciate the light on our path.

Remember to appreciate the moment you are in. When you live in the past or for the future, you miss everything in between, and you will have never truly lived.

Remember to take a new path home today. You may learn something new that will change you forever.

Remember that change is a good thing. When you learn new things and take on new challenges, you expand your mind and become a better person for it.

Remember that if you love someone, tell them. Life is short and it moves very quickly. Loving someone openly gives purpose and meaning to your days.

Remember to stop and take a breath. Life is not a race to be won. The only way to enjoy all of it is one moment at a time.

Rebecca Finkelstein

I'm Here if
You Need Me

Being a teenager is about
discovering what you stand for,
choosing how to act,
and learning who you are.
It can be confusing,
and sometimes
you'll make mistakes.
None of us is perfect,
but I believe you'll do just fine.

You are a thoughtful
and caring person,
and I'm always glad to listen
and to help you
whenever you want me to.

—————————

Lydia S. Ure

What I Want
to Give to You...

My time when you need someone
to listen or stand with you.
My heart when you need someone
to care.
My support when you need to know
what a great person you are.
My faith in you,
in your goals and dreams,
and your ability to achieve them.
My perspective for when you are
confused and want another opinion.
My strength for when the path
you walk seems all uphill,
and you need to rest a bit.
My understanding when you make
mistakes or you don't live up
to your own expectations,
and you need to know that
you don't have to be perfect.

Most of all,
I give you my heart always,
for the bond between us
is unconditional.

———————————

Ruthann Tholen

Be Positive
in Your Attitude

There is nothing more powerful in this world than a positive attitude. It will see you through the best and the worst of times, and reassure you when nothing else seems to.

A positive outlook arms you with the confidence you need to reach for your dreams, no matter how high they are.

If you take chances in life, what you're really telling yourself is that you believe in who you are.

Remember to tell yourself that you can do whatever you set your mind to — and you'll see just how far that kind of thinking will get you.

—————

T. L. Nash

Have Confidence in
Your Choices

Life is full of choices,
and not all of them come with ease.
In most cases, there can be
    more than one answer,
and too often, knowing what
    the wisest one will be
is, at best, uncertain.
Perhaps it's so difficult to choose
because there are so many roads
    leading to the same destination.
Each one has its own unique lessons
    and experiences along the way.
On one hand, life is too short
    to not rush forward
and take hold of it with both hands.
Yet there's a lot to be said for
    savoring the moment
and exploring all the options.
Important decisions take time
    and consideration,
and they are seldom easy to make.
Some of them take the past and the future
    into consideration,
and others have to go by blind faith
    and instinct.
The important thing is to have the confidence
to do what is ultimately best for you,
and to go for what you really want.

———————————

Barbara Cage

LEARN FROM MISTAKES...

As you make your way to the places where dreams come true, don't be afraid to make mistakes. They are lessons that teach you how to do better. If you seize these opportunities to learn about life, mistakes will lead you to new and exciting places where you'll find beautiful things.

Jacqueline Schiff

Mistakes are steppingstones upon which we build our future. With each one we gain insight and courage, learn something new, and rise a little closer to the sunshine. Then we begin again.

Elle Mastro

...AND KEEP MOVING FORWARD

---◇◇◇---

Always remember to have faith in the things that you do. Even when you get a little discouraged, don't allow yourself to give up. Only when you have done your very best can you stop and say to yourself, "I tried," and that's what matters most.

If you back away from obstacles that appear before you because they seem too difficult, then you're not being true to yourself. Don't be afraid to take risks, or even to fail. It isn't about winning or losing. It's about loving yourself enough and believing in who you are that counts in the end.

T. L. Nash

FAILURE IS A
STEPPINGSTONE...

———◇◇◇———

"Failure." It's only a word.
But it carries with it so much pain
     and so little concern,
so much frustration
     and so little respect,
so much stress and so little
     understanding
that people spend their lives
     running through their days
in the hope of avoiding the long arm
     of this little word.

To test your vision, you must risk
     failure.

To temper your ego, you must attempt
     the impossible.

To tell your story, you must
     take a chance.

...ON THE ROAD TO SUCCESS

To see beyond the horizon, you must
spread your wings.

To be all you can be, you must
stretch, flex, try, and go beyond
your proven limits.

To bridge the silence, you must risk
rejection.

To advance into the unknown, you must
risk the peril of all your
previous beliefs and emotions
that feel so secure.

Failure is not negative. It is a teacher.
It molds, refines, and polishes you
so that one day your light will
shine for all to see.

It isn't the failure you experience
that will determine your destiny,
but your next step and then the next
that will tell
the story of your life.

Tim Connor

Ten Ways to Avoid Discouragement

1. Look at life as a journey and enjoy the ride. Get the most out of the detours and realize they're sometimes necessary.

2. Do your best, but if what you've been doing has caused you discouragement, try a different approach. Be passionate about the process, but don't be so attached to the outcome.

3. Wish the best for everyone, with no personal strings attached. Applaud someone else's win as much as you would your own.

4. Trust that there's a divine plan, that we don't always know what's best for us. A disappointment now could mean a victory later, so don't be disappointed. There is usually a reason.

5. Ask no more of yourself than the best that you can do, and be satisfied with that. Be compassionate toward yourself as well as others. Know your calling, your gift, and do it well.

6. Don't worry about something after it's done;
   it's out of your hands then, too late, over!
   Learn the lesson and move on.

7. Have the attitude that no one, except you,
   owes you anything. Give without expecting
   a thank-you in return. But when someone
   does something for you, be appreciative of
   even the smallest gesture.

8. Choose your thoughts or your thoughts will
   choose you; they will free you or keep you
   bound. Educate your spirit and give it
   authority over your feelings.

9. Judge no one, and disappointment and
   forgiveness won't be an issue. No one can
   let you down if you're not leaning on them.
   People can't hurt you unless you allow
   them to.

10. Love anyway... for no reason... and give...
    just because.

———————————
Donna Fargo

Little by Little,
I Know I Have to Let
You Go

I remember staring at your
   perfect little features
and feeling thrilled at each new sound
   and expression.
A fierce need to protect you
   came over me then,
and it has never gone away.
When you were a child,
I was able to hold you close
   through illness and heartache.
I could hold your hand as you faced
   new experiences,
and my presence and guidance seemed to
assure you of a certain level of safety.

But little by little, I have had to let you go
and allow you to make your own way.
So often I wanted to call you back
    and have you stay
in the protective circle of my arms.
I never wanted you to have to face injury
    or heartache,
yet I knew that you had to in order to grow.
Now you continue to grow
and make your own decisions.
You often face life alone.
Just remember that no matter what,
    I love you.
I could never stop loving you.
You are the hugs and smiles from my past,
    the hopes and dreams of my future.

Barbara Cage

Being a Parent
Is Not Always Easy

Being a parent is not always easy. I sometimes forget that being a teenager isn't easy either, and that growing up can be difficult and confusing.

I get so caught up in being the perfect parent that I sometimes forget there are no perfect children. In my quest to create the "ideal" child, I forget the amount of pressure I put on you to meet my standards.

In my effort to make life better for you than it was for me, I sometimes do all the talking and fail to listen to any of your ideas. I expect you to learn from my mistakes without experiencing any of your own. I find it easier to keep you grounded than to allow you to spread your wings and fly.

Sometimes I don't see your tears or say I'm sorry for the pain that I unknowingly cause you. I forget that your problems and worries are at least as big as mine, if not bigger. When you fall off the pedestal I place you on, I don't realize how far down it is.

I'm telling you now that I'm sorry for not being more sensitive to your feelings. I'm not perfect, and I won't expect you to be, either. Together, let's work on the imperfections until we are satisfied with each other. Above all else, remember that I love you.

Elizabeth Ann Nichols

I Couldn't Have Asked for a Better Child

I don't have the same fun with anyone else that I have with you. I love laughing with you and sharing the humor that seems uniquely ours. I'm proud of you, too. You have a kind heart; you're thoughtful and nice, regardless of the circumstances or who you are with. Your love of others, and the way you freely show it, touches my heart.

Besides being a wonderful child, you are also a great friend. You often help me see things in a new way, and your advice is sound and logical. You have a humbleness and gentleness about you, but you also know what you want out of life and work hard to get it.

You accept yourself and those around you. You've gone through some trying and difficult times, but you've learned from them — which turns them into valuable experiences that will make you wiser and more understanding.

You are usually content and happy, and that makes you an easy, enjoyable person to be around. There isn't anyone anywhere who could ever have blessed my life like you have. I love you.

Barbara Cage

Be the Person
You Are
Meant to Be

Don't ever be afraid to be who you are.
Don't keep yourself from expressing love,
kindness, and patience. Don't cut yourself
off from the things that nourish your soul.
Live in the spirit of life; there are no walls
to keep you captive. You are as beautiful
as you choose to be.

Take a step you have not dared to take
before — a leap of faith, a stride in a new
direction. Discover a new creation within
yourself. When you think you have reached
an end, watch for life to take a turn and
renew itself. Remember that irritations
often produce a pearl; your shortcomings
become your strengths. May you find yourself
like a seed when springtime comes, and grow
in your own season.

Do not try to change who you are;
change the way you look at things.
Expand your viewpoint. Be aware of
the new directions that open every
minute. Like a conductor, you can
direct a chorus of many circumstances
to create a harmonious life. Assume
responsibility for whatever life sends
your way. Be victorious in the way
you respond to everything that happens
to you. Live on the great ocean of
possibilities, and sail away toward
your dreams. _____

Tanya P. Shubin

Dream Great Dreams

Many people speak of dreams as fanciful things like fairies and charmed rings and lands of enchantment. Others only believe in faraway dreams such as stars or sea castles with elf-like inhabitants. There are day dreamers and night dreamers who dream up make-believe places. They use imagination, and in that are dream-gifted. But the serious dreamers are those who catch dreams to bring them to life, and show that when they were dreaming, they meant it.

Ashley Rice

Child of mine...
Sing to the stars; tell them your secrets.
Dream great dreams
And don't be afraid to chase them.
Live boldly. Love passionately.
Stand on your toes and tickle the sky...

Throw yourself into the world;
Be brave but not foolish.
Expect no more from others
Than you are willing to give.
Be generous with your talents, your time,
And your heart.

Never fear being your best;
Know that to me you already are.
Above all, know this:
Should ever you fall, my love will catch you
And bring you safely home.

———————————
Kathy Larson

Never Forget What Is
Most Important

It's not having everything go right;
it's facing whatever goes wrong.
It's not being without fear;
it's having the determination
   to go on in spite of it.
What's important is not
   where you stand,
but the direction you're going in.
It's more than never having bad moments;
   it's knowing you are always
   bigger than the moment.
It's believing you have already
   been given everything
you need to handle life.

It's not being able to rid
    the world of all its injustices;
it's being able to rise above them.

It's the belief in your heart
    that there will always be
more good than bad in the world.
Remember to live just this one day
and not add tomorrow's troubles
    to today's load.
Remember that every day ends
and brings a new tomorrow
full of exciting new things.
Love what you do,
    do the best you can,
and always remember
    how much you are loved.

———————
Vickie M. Worsham

My Love Is
With You... Always

You are my teenager, my child, my gift that was given so wonderfully. But you are also your own person, your own special blend of so many qualities; a magnificent combination of feelings, hopes, thoughts, and dreams.

You are creative and caring and filled with life. But I know, too, that the world isn't always fair to you. In the tough times of life, when the days aren't going the way you'd like them to, I want you to remember, always, please: that you can always turn to me.

I want to be a place you can come to...
for shelter, for unconditional caring, for
sharing all the support one person can
give. I want to be a person you can turn
to, for answers and understanding, or just
to reinforce the feeling of how incredibly
special you are.

I want to do everything I possibly can for
you because that's what love does when it
is strong and grateful and giving. I want you
to know what a gift it is to be your parent,

and that my love for you...
is never-ending.

Douglas Pagels

ACKNOWLEDGMENTS

We gratefully acknowledge the permission granted by the following authors, publishers, and authors' representatives to reprint poems or excerpts from their publications.

Sue Gillies-Bradley for "There is beauty in so many unrecognized places." Copyright © 2003 by Sue Gillies-Bradley. All rights reserved.

Amy Oscar for "Instead of trying to fit yourself...." Copyright © 2003 by Amy Oscar. All rights reserved.

Jacqueline Schiff for "You must always love yourself" and "As you make your way...." Copyright © 2003 by Jacqueline Schiff. All rights reserved.

Linda Sackett-Morrison for "A family is people joined in love." Copyright © 2003 by Linda Sackett-Morrison. All rights reserved.

Barbara J. Hall for "There's no greater place on earth...." Copyright © 2003 by Barbara J. Hall. All rights reserved.

Susan Hickman Sater for "Remember that home will always be home...." Copyright © 2003 by Susan Hickman Sater. All rights reserved.

Barbara Cage for "Have Confidence in Your Choices" and "I Couldn't Have Asked for a Better Child." Copyright © 2003 by Barbara Cage. All rights reserved.

James E. Smith for "The World Changed the Day You Were Born." Copyright © 2003 by James E. Smith. All rights reserved.

Rebecca Finkelstein for "Words to Remember..." Copyright © 2003 by Rebecca Finkelstein. All rights reserved.

Lydia S. Ure for "I'm Here If You Need Me." Copyright © 2003 by Lydia S. Ure. All rights reserved.

T. L. Nash for "Be Positive in Your Attitude." Copyright © 2003 by T. L. Nash. All rights reserved.

Tim Connor for "Failure Is a Steppingstone..." Copyright © 1994 by Tim Connor. All rights reserved.

PrimaDonna Entertainment Corp. for "Ten Ways to Avoid Discouragement" by Donna Fargo. Copyright © 2003 by PrimaDonna Entertainment Corp. All rights reserved.

Elizabeth Ann Nichols for "Being a Parent Is Not Always Easy." Copyright © 2003 by Elizabeth Ann Nichols. All rights reserved.

Tanya P. Shubin for "Be the Person You Are Meant to Be." Copyright © 2003 by Tanya P. Shubin. All rights reserved.

Kathy Larson for "Child of mine...." Copyright © 2003 by Kathy Larson. All rights reserved.

Vickie M. Worsham for "Never Forget What Is Most Important." Copyright © 2003 by Vickie M. Worsham. All rights reserved.

A careful effort has been made to trace the ownership of selections used in this anthology in order to obtain permission to reprint copyrighted material and give proper credit to the copyright owners. If any error or omission has occurred, it is completely inadvertent, and we would like to make corrections in future editions provided that written notification is made to the publisher:

. BLUE MOUNTAIN ARTS, INC., P.O. Box 4549, Boulder, Colorado 80306.